Declutter Guide: How to Organize your Life in 2 Weeks or Less

Organizing Tips to Simplify Your Life

By Ariel Benet Savant

Declutter Guide: How to Organize Your Life in 2 Weeks or Less - Organizing Tips to Simplify Your Life.

Copyright © 2015 by Sovereign Education Media–All Rights Reserved.

No part of this book may be reproduced in any form without permission in writing from the author. Reviewers may quote brief passages in reviews.

No part of this publication may be reproduced in any written, electronic, recording, photocopying, or by any information storage and retrieval system, or transmitted by email without written permission from the publisher. Respective authors own all copyrights not held by the publisher.

Although every precaution has been taken to verify the accuracy of the information contained herein, the author and publisher assume no responsibilities for any errors or omissions, or contrary interpretations of the subject matter herein.

Disclaimer
The information herein is offered for informational and educational purposes solely and should not be taken as expert instruction. The reader is responsible for his or her own actions. The information provided herein is stated to be truthful and consistent. Under no circumstances will any legal responsibility or blame be held against the publisher or author for any reparation, damages, or monetary loss due to the information herein, either directly or indirectly.

ISBN – 978-0-9995775-5-4
Library of Congress Control Number : 2020905838

Publisher: Sovereign Education Media
332 S. Michigan Avenue #121-A850
Chicago, IL. 60604 USA
Sovereigneducationmedia.com
312 685-2788

Jacket Design: German Creative
Cover Design: Ravsingh Designs

Table of Contents

Introduction vii

Section 1: Stuff......It Blows the Life Out of YOU!!!........ 1
    Why "Stuff" Can Blow the Life from You 1
    How Did This Happen To Me? 6
    Reduce Stress and Be Productive 15
    Clutter in Review! 20

Section 2: Week 1 – Your Home & Your Work Space..... 21
    The Living Spaces 23
    The Living Room/Family room 26
    The Kitchen 27
    Bedrooms 32
    Closets & Drawers 34
    Home office / Desk 37
    Review Week 1 – Section 2 41

Section 3: Week 2 - Your Finances And Your Life 43
    Shred & Ditch the Paper 44
    Bill Consolidation 46

Automate Savings & Start-Up Bill Pay..................50
Commitments..................51
Routines..................53
Computer..................57
Digital Clutter..................58
Week 3 Review..................61

Section 4: The Long Haul..................**63**
Create Central Locations..................63
Put Things In Their Place..................64
Clean Regularly – Especially The Hot Spots..................66
Recycle & Donate..................66
Keep Up On Expiration Dates..................67

Conclusion..................70

About the Author..................75

PICK UP YOUR FREE GIFTS
https://dl.bookfunnel.com/2dximykla1

First, I'd like to thank you for downloading the book, ***Declutter Guide–How to organize your Life in 2 Weeks or less: Organizing tips to simplify your life.***

As a way of saying thank you for your purchase, the author has created a Free Bonus booklet which and important information that will help to make the process more efficient. You'll want to get your hands on your handy-printable PDF's right away. You'll be glad you did. You'll also get a copy of her latest release – **Present Moment – The Art of Authentic Living.**

**Be sure to visit
https://dl.bookfunnel.com/2dximykla1**

Introduction

Have you ever been so exhausted that you felt as though you have gone through the day and haven't accomplished a single thing? Or maybe you have tried to sit down to work and feel like you can't concentrate? Have you ever gone looking for something and thought you knew exactly where it was, but ended up spending a lot of time trying to locate what you were looking for? Or maybe you just feel you no longer have time to do the things you enjoy?

If you ever had any of these feelings, you may be experiencing stress from the clutter in your life. Having an excess of things in your life can cause distractions and create feelings of stress and anxiety.

The good news is that by learning to declutter your life you can start reaping the rewards such as:

1. Increase in productivity
2. Spend less time cleaning and dusting

3. Increased clarity and focus

4. The ability to find things more quickly

5. Become less attached to stuff in general

6. Create more time to do things you enjoy

I grew up in a very organized home. As a teenager I was always attracted to lifestyle and interior design magazines. My mom had a friend who was a professional organizer. During college I was lucky to have two internships, one in my major and another one was with her organizing company. Over the years I picked up a lot of tips and tricks I use in our homes. My friends have begged me to share those tips with them and now I am compelled to share them with you. So if you want to declutter your life...read on! Best of all you can do it in 2 weeks or less!

Believe it or not you can have a life where you are in complete control of your time and you can start now! The process of decluttering is a journey and this is the first step. You must first identify the purpose of decluttering......Why?? If you don't take the time to do this, you can repeatedly make the same mistakes again.

In this book you will learn to identify the things that are cluttering your life, learn how to rid yourself of that clutter, and learn how to keep yourself from cluttering up your life again!

<u>Who this book is for:</u>

- Someone that has a hard time keeping their living spaces clean
- A person who is extremely active and on the go but disorganized
- A person who feels overwhelmed by their office
- Someone who cleans but feels they are not making progress
- Feeling overwhelmed at home and frequently can't find things
- Feeling embarrassed to have people over due to a messy environment

This book is also for anyone who desires to live a purposeful and more organized life with greater intention. You need to congratulate yourself for taking a huge step to change your life. Now it's time to get started. Thanks again for downloading this book, and I hope you enjoy it.

Ariel Benet Savant

Be sure to visit my website for bonuses and updates @ arielbenetsavant.com

SECTION 1

Stuff......It Blows the Life Out of YOU!!!

Why "Stuff" Can Blow the Life from You

As a starting point, you need to understand that clutter can profoundly affect how you live day to day. Your personal space is a direct reflection of your mental health picture, and your mental health picture is a direct reflection of your personal space. How we choose to fill our personal spaces will determine how we feel from day to day.

When we are feeling less than "right" it is important to take a hard look at the environment that we are keeping ourselves in both physically and mentally. If our personal space is cluttered and filled with "stuff", it could very well be the reason we are feeling disorganized, chaotic and drained. There are several ways that clutter or "stuff" can drain the life out of you. It can negatively affect the way you process or filter information, keep you from engaging in creative thought, and leave you feeling tired with low energy.

Humans are notoriously horrible with multitasking. Everyone feels they are getting more accomplished when they are doing multiple things at once; however science has proven this method slows us down. Research has proven that working on a single task is far more efficient than directing our energy in several directions.

This is related to why clutter has such a negative effect on our mental capacities. When you see a cluttered desk at home or the office, it simply places an added load on the brain which expends additional mental resources to process. Using all this mental power requires energy, which is why clutter often can make you feel so exhausted.

Your Personal Space

A disorganized space can negatively affect how you focus and how you process information. How many times have you had to reread instructions because you read them but had no idea what they said? Or maybe you start working on an important project only to find that you are side tracked and are working on a completely different project than what you started with?

The fact of the matter is, a disorganized space can cause you to jump from task to task without completing anything. Another research study scientifically proved that having things around you that do not serve a specific purpose, or better known as "clutter", can interfere with the way your brain filters and manages the information you receive. When clutter affects the way you focus and process information it can lead to feelings of disorientation, chaos, and confusion. These feelings are directly related to stress.

Blocking Your Creativity

Another way clutter can suck the life from you is when it becomes a barrier for your creative thought. When your senses become overloaded, you are no longer able to use them to experience the world around you. Doing too many things at once or spreading yourself too thin can keep you from problem solving or deductive reasoning.

When this happens, you are no longer able to think of ways to handle situations that may arise, and must rely on your instincts or previous experiences to get through. When your creative thought process is inhibited, you may also find that you are no longer able to express yourself effectively and find it difficult to come up with new or innovative solutions. This can lead to states of confusion, anger, and frustration. These are all emotions that drain you and can cause you to feel inadequate.

When You Lose Time and Money

Finally, the stuff in your life can drain you of time and energy. Disorganization in your personal space can leave you scattered. Not knowing where the things you need are located and having to spend time searching is definitely a drain on your time. While the stuff in your life is not necessarily all material items, other time and energy draining clutter can be things like:

- your finances
- files on your computer
- digital clutter
- your email
- notifications from your phone.

Anything that takes your focus from the task at hand is clutter. What is worse is that we tend to give importance to this clutter and allow it to be distracting.

How many times do you avoid going to your e-mail because you have thousands of newsletters and sales pitches on a daily basis. You mean to clean it out but now it is overwhelming and you avoid it. Or what about when you hear the "ping" of your computer notifying you of a social media post and you get lost on Facebook or Twitter for hours? Even a text message can consistently drag you from the things you need to do. You also have to watch out for over-committing with too many "to-do's" on your calendar, this can be time and energy draining.

Clutter overstimulates our senses causing distractions and making you spend too much time on things that are unnecessary or unimportant. It can make it more difficult to relax, both physically and mentally because the clutter in your life is a constant reminder that you have a lot of things to do keeping you from the things you enjoy.

Clutter causes anxiety because cleaning, sorting and arranging, and the thought of it, is mentally draining. Clutter can also cause a sense of embarrassment when your personal space is not ready for visitors.

Most often we are not in tune to the signs that "stuff" or "clutter" is consuming us. The clutter is a part of our everyday lives. It hides in our closets and under our beds. It disguises itself as part of our job or daily routines. However, if we were to take a very close look at some tell-tale signs in our behaviors, we would start to notice that we are indeed having the life sucked out of us by our "stuff".

How Did This Happen To Me?

This is a question anyone who is consumed by clutter asks themselves, how did this happen to me? The answer is very simple. You gather and collect material things all the time. And when you do this you develop an attachment. Now the attachment can look different for different objects. It may be emotional or financial. But these attachments are what keep you from ridding yourself of the stuff that drains you.

Physical Pain

Believe it or not, when you are thinking of getting rid of items you have attached yourself to, you may actually experience pain. Yes, that is right, physical pain. Researchers at Yale have discovered that your brain triggers in an area which lets you know that something is wrong when you are ridding yourself of something that you have attached yourself to. When you have developed such an attachment, your brain tells you that you are experiencing physical pain.

Often times the pain may be undetectable but other times it may be very noticeable. The pain you experience could be as small as a paper cut or as prominent as stubbing your toe, but the fact remains, you may hurt or feel discomfort. This same reaction or trigger keeps us from buying things we think are too expensive or gives us the feeling that something will "someday" have a potential value. It allows us to rationalize the act of keeping the object. In some cases, it can be extreme as the rationalization for hoarders that the item is necessary for their survival. Here are some reasons you hold on to items and have difficulty letting go:

- the money you spent
- it could have sentimental value

- it could be the result of a major life change
- it could be in your life due to low self-esteem
- depression or lack of personal boundaries
- it could also be clutter due to poor time management or planning

To better understand where yours comes from you will need to see what the types of clutter look like and how they affect you personally. Only then will you be able to make the mind shift change necessary to regain control of your life.

Financial Attachment

One of the most prominent reasons we hang onto our clutter is a financial attachment. You spend money on the things you buy. As an individual in our society we have come to realize that we work hard for our money. Hard working people think it is in poor judgement to spend money on something they do not need. So you make a rationalization for keeping things.

Perhaps you have purchased items that your upbringing would lead you to believe is a luxury item, and you are proud to have been able to make that purchase. You rationalize that getting rid of it may bring shame because it was extravagant. You also would like to believe that you are a socially conscious being. Financially and socially it is in bad form to waste money. How hard would it be to say you made a mistake and should not have purchased an item because it was a waste of hard earned money and then just throw or give it away?

Emotional Attachment

Sentimental attachment to items in your personal space is an emotional attachment that you may have formed. Maybe you are keeping things from your past such as:

- old clothes that you wore in high school
- an ex's sweatshirt
- boxes of school work from your kids
- grown children's favorite toys from when they were little
- boxes of things from a loved one that has passed on that just sit in the corner unused.

The items that you have developed a sentimental attachment to are the hardest to get rid of. Often times you feel guilt over the thought that they are unneeded or harder yet, they are unwanted.

Life Changes

Life changes tend to bring an overabundance of clutter or stuff into our lives. The clutter or stuff from life events may also bring feelings of sentiment and guilt when it is time to clean up. Life events that may lead to feelings of sentimental or obligational guilt:

- weddings
- divorce
- graduations
- death
- the birth or death of a child
- monumental birthday events, or anniversaries.

Other life changes may bring on clutter but tend to be easier to handle such as a family relocation or new home.

Emotional Afflictions

Emotional afflictions such as low self-esteem, depression, and lack of personal boundaries can also lead to debilitating clutter. Low self-esteem is a huge generator of clutter or stuff. This psychological ailment leads you to believe that you will look better, feel better or be better with more clothes, shoes, ties, suits or "stuff". Here is where the old saying "he with the most toys wins" comes into play. Maybe your clutter is from another saying "keeping up with the Joneses".

Depression

Low self-esteem is often linked with depression. Depression is dangerous because it creates a cycle between clutter and anxiety. Anxiety or depression about yourself and your place in life can lead to the inability or lack of desire to clean or pick up. This results in a messy unpresentable space, which creates more anxiety and depression. Clutter in this respect robs you of the ability to enjoy the activities that make you happy by filling you with guilt or making you feel like you have no time to enjoy them.

There is scientific evidence between high-stress levels in female homeowners and clutter which does not affect men in the same way. Men did not seem to be bothered by the mess which can lead to a build-up of tension in the relationship. Most women in the study associate having a clean and well-organized home with a successful family.

In the United States consumers buy 40% of the world's toys, yet we only bear 3% of the world's children. Research has shown that in many homes parents spend a lot of discretionary money on children's toys. These toys take up a lot of space in the home not just the child's room.

Scientists have discovered that the roots of this are parents who feel guilty about not spending more time with their children. These feelings of guilt add to the depression and the cycle of anxiety. Having a lack of personal boundaries also fall into this category.

You may be harboring stowaways in your personal space. Keeping personal items for friends or family in any of your personal spaces can create anxiety for someone with any of these psychological limitations.

Personal spaces include your bedroom, closet, under your bed, spare room or even your garage. This book doesn't cover all the psychological issues in depth. However if you feel you need additional support in this area, you can visit http://www.adaa.org

Poor Planning or Time Management

The last way you may accumulate clutter in your life may be due to poor planning or time management. Clutter is not always physical. Sometimes it may come in the form of time consumption. This clutter may appear as things that steal your time like over-committing to appointments and activities. It could also mean time sucking activities such as social media, and immediately responding to the constant distraction of incoming text messages.

Identifying your clutter areas can help give you clues as to corresponding places you may be experiencing discord in your life. Take a look at the following chart to see if you can identify your clutter culprits.

Home vs. Work –Clutter in the doorway of your home can be an indicator that you have difficulty making the transition between work and home. It may also indicate that you are blocking the outside world from entering your home.

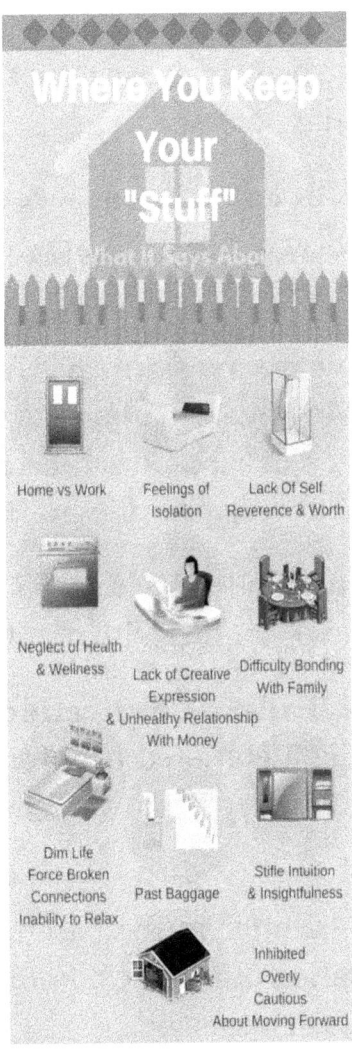

http://weorganizeu.com/clutter-hot-spot-reveal/

Feelings of Isolation – Clutter in your living room may be an indication of family discord or that you may be hiding yourself from the world.

Lack of Self Reverence & Worth – A cluttered bathroom may indicate body image, lack of self-confidence or a feeling of not being safe.

Neglect of Health & Wellness – A cluttered kitchen can indicate a neglect of nourishing your body or spirit. It can also show a lack of emotional support or self-control.

Lack of Creative Expression & Unhealthy Relationship with Money – An unorganized office or desk can be an indication of a lack of self-accountability and a lax sense of home & work priorities.

Difficulty Bonding With Family – A cluttered dining room can be a sign of conflict with family & friends.

Dim Life Force Broken Connections/ Inability to Relax – Generally a cluttered bedroom with excessive stuff shows that intimacy is not valued or there is sleep deprivation.

Past Baggage – Clutter in the basement indicates issues in the foundation of a home pointing directly to not being able to let go of baggage.

Stifle Intuition & Insightfulness – Stuff things down deep if there is clutter in your closet.

Inhibited Overly Cautious About Moving Forward – Garage clutter is a blocking of independence.

Reduce Stress and Be Productive

Decluttering your life or getting rid of unnecessary stuff definitely has benefits in your life. Now just to be clear, decluttering doesn't mean getting organized or investing in storage containers and decorative furniture in order to hide what you have. To truly declutter your life you must get rid of the things in your life that are not necessary or of no use.

Let's take a look at how your life will improve once you get rid of the excess.

- **Time for Self–Care** – With a less cluttered environment you will have more time to care for yourself properly. You will be less likely to neglect your physical health, exercise and have the ability to care for your spiritual well-being.

- **Time For Self-Fulfilment** – Without the constant stress of a to-do list you will have time to engage in the activities that bring you pleasure or enjoyment. You'll have time to watch a movie or read a book.

- **More Money** – Now with the ability to discern between necessary and just a fun item to buy, you will ultimately spend less.

- **Your Home Will Be More Appealing & Restful** – With less clutter in your home you will find you are more comfortable, will enjoy being at home and will be able to settle down and relax.

- **You Will Experience More Discipline From Self & Family** – With set routines and places to put things you will find that your family will learn to follow suit. With the new routines your family will have more responsibility for upkeep of your home. They will take on pride of ownership of their home and you will no longer be exclusively responsible for your home any longer.

- **Starting young is the key**–It's never too early. When toddlers beg to help fold laundry or wash the car with us it's easier to send them off to play so we can get the job done quickly ourselves. But this is exactly the time to foster a child's natural helpfulness. By engaging the child in tasks, it also promotes positive development in many areas.

- **Research shows** – Children who participated in household tasks starting at age three or four were likely to succeed as an adult such as meeting career goals, high educational accomplishments, and maintaining positive relationships. Waiting until the children are older can often backfire. It may take some convincing and be very challenging to involve teenagers to help clean if they had little exposure to it. Taking turns and working together as a family can help strengthen relationships with each other.

- **More Space** – Removing the clutter will free up space that can readily be used for other activities.

- **Freedom for Creative Thought** – With fewer distractions you will be able to concentrate and engage in critical thinking, problem solving, and dreaming about the future.

- **More Energy** – Once you are no longer solely responsible for the care, running, and upkeep of your home you will find you have more energy to engage in other activities that seemed to expend your energy and drain you. You may even find enjoyment in those activities.

- **Sense of Accomplishment** – Decluttering a home and life is a life-altering undertaking. The sense of fulfillment and accomplishment you will experience is liberating.

- **Helping Others** – The items you remove from your home may be donated to homeless shelters, teen homes, or organizations to help those in need.

- **Make a Bit of Money** – Those items that you remove as clutter can be made into a yard sale or a consignment shop.

- **More Opportunity for Socialization** – With an uncluttered home there is more opportunity for socialization without embarrassment or guilt.

- **More Productive** – Decluttering allows you to focus and get more accomplished with fewer distractions.

- **More Romance** – Having a clean sanctuary you will open the door to more relaxed feelings and be able to ignite romantic evenings in a space without hindrances allowing you to enjoy the time.

- **Long Lost Memories** – By decluttering you will find the memories that you truly want to hang on to.

- **More Valuable Belongings** – By having fewer belongings you will begin to place a strong and higher value on caring for the ones you have.

- **Freedom** – Decluttering gives you freedom. It allows you to schedule your time without over-committing yourself.

- **More Organized** – Decluttering will give everything a place. You will no longer go hunting for the items you need giving you in turn time and energy without the stress.

- **Safer Home** – By lessening the items in your home you have created a cleaner environment to live in. There is less chance of accidents and illness.

- **Become Healthier** – An orderly home without stuff or clutter allows for a healthier environment. There are fewer places for bacteria and germs to hide and less waste. Your home will bring less opportunity for allergens and illness.

- **Sleep Better Less Worry** – A clean and decluttered environment creates a calm relaxing atmosphere which in turn allows you to relax and have restful and productive sleep.

- **Able To Handle Situations As They Arise** – With a clear head and mind from a clean and orderly life you will be able to react to daily events calmly without anxiety.

Clutter in Review!

Have you identified why you clutter? Here is a quick review:

- There is a financial investment
- There is an emotional attachment
- A life change or life changes have occurred
- Possible emotional afflictions
- Poor planning
- Digital overload

Now it is time to ask yourself will you continue to live your life as it is or are you willing to continue on to break from your clutter and improve your life?

The choice is yours and you can have a better life in 2 weeks or less!

SECTION 2

Week 1 – Your Home & Your Work Space

In order to get started it is necessary to get some things ready in order to declutter. Be sure you have the following items on hand:

- **Garbage Bags** – if you have a lot of clutter you will need to be sure you have plenty on hand

- **Magic markers and labels**

- **Totes and Boxes** – Make sure to have enough totes or boxes available with containers marked "Donate", "Good Condition –Consignment Shop", "Throw Away".

- **A Close Friend or Family Members** – If you have a habit of getting distracted make sure you have someone to keep you focused. Remember you are still new at this.

- **Music** – Funny that you are trying to get rid of distractions, but you need a distraction which will help keep you in the mood. Put on music that is uplifting and makes you feel good.

- **Get A Timer** – You need to set a time limit to meet your goals.

- **Ask yourself these Questions**:

Is this trash?

Do I use this…If it's been more than 6 months (donate, find a consignment shop and sell it, or throw it out)

Do I LOVE it? Does it make me feel good?

- **Here are a few tips to help you on your journey.**

    1. Move quickly and swiftly through the process for each room

    2. Make sure you stick to the time you have set for each section

    3. Once you have made a decision about an item stick to it, don't second guess yourself

    4. Be sure to keep everything neat as you go, don't make a bigger mess

5. Keep in mind what the room is being used for when you start to clear the "stuff".

The Living Spaces

Start by identifying each living space in your home and assigning a work day of the week to declutter that space. You can set up a limited time to do this late in the evening after everyone has settled in, or schedule the time using some of the accrued days off from work, "use it or lose it". For example this is the schedule for week one:

A. Living Room – Monday

B. Kitchen/Pantry – Tuesday

C. Bathrooms – Wednesday

D. Bedrooms – Thursday

E. Closets / Home Office –Friday

F. Basement/Garage – Saturday

G. Attic/Spare Storage room –Sunday

Remember that each room has a purpose. There is literally no right or wrong way to declutter. You can read a million books on the topic and each book will have different suggestions on how to start. When you set your timer and budget your time accordingly for each space you can accomplish a great deal. The timer limits set in the example are simply sample times to get you moving and a reminder to not linger. Every space is different, for example your closet may be extremely large so you will have to adjust the time limits accordingly.

Be sure that when you go through the room you are sure that items that remain in the room are meant to be there. For example, laundry baskets don't belong in the living room, and the children's toys don't belong in your bedroom. Make sure that the items in the rooms are appropriate to be used in that room.

Here is a simple and quick process for making it through your living spaces and quickly decluttering rooms so you are free to do the things you want.

1. Take a garbage bag and set your timer for 15 minutes. Go quickly through the room and pick up all the trash in the room and place it in the bag. This includes newspapers & magazines you have already read. Anything that should go in the garbage should go directly in the bag.

2. Now take a bin big enough to hold books, trays, clothes, dishes, toys, and anything that does not belong in the room. Set your timer for 15 minutes. Once again, go through the room and pick up anything that is out of place and place it in the bin. Remember to move swiftly so that you don't second guess yourself.

3. You will also have large bins in the middle of the floor marked "Donate" and "Consignment Shop". Go through the bin of unsorted items and place everything in the donated bin that is no longer used or doesn't make you feel good. Set aside everything that is broken. Make a decision to toss it or if it is not too bad, it can be donated.

4. Next, set the timer for 15 minutes and go through the room and return everything to its proper place. Restack books, place remotes in one place, fold blankets, reorganize cords, and wipe things down.

5. Visually divide your room into four sections. Take a tote with you and go to the first section. Set your timer for 20 minutes. Go through the first section and look at the items on the shelves and tables. Look for items that you have not used in at least a month. Rid the section of anything that has no use or that you may have been holding onto just in case you might need it and get rid of it. Once you determined it goes in the bin do not take it out and try to make use of it.

6. Repeat this process for the other three sections of the room.

The Living Room/Family room

Create a Play zone

If toys are taking over your family room, it's time to get organized. Take a look at your living room/family room and transform unused corners into a small play area. Corners are a great space to add a small bookcase or children's table. Encourage your children to pick up after he or she is playing and hold them accountable.

Remember, perfection is never a reasonable goal

Just think about it, small habits of cleaning your space before you leave can make a big difference when it comes to having a calm and uncluttered home. For some people, spending a small amount of time on one project or space is less frustrating. Find a place for everything and take it there. Once you have determined that an item is going to be donated to charity, a local shelter, or to be thrown out, take it there as soon as possible. Don't get in the habit of accumulating bags and bins of items in your home.

The overall goal is to set up a space that works well for your needs. Keep in mind you don't have to live in an empty home but evaluate what you can live with and without is important. You want a home that is welcoming, warm, and filled with treasures that you love and make you feel good.

The Kitchen

Refrigerator

This is the most time consuming of the tasks. It takes the most time because often things become buried. The best way to handle the refrigerator is very systematically. Start with the big project and then move to the smaller.

- Set your timer for ninety minutes for this task. Remember to move quickly. It may seem like it is a lot of time, but it actually is not.

- Remove everything from the shelves and place them on the counters. Go through and toss expired foods. The most common ones are salad dressings and sauces. Do not keep anything that is within 2 weeks of the expiration date.

- Next take to your shelves and wipe them down. Start by making sure your shelves are the proper height.

This seems odd to mention, but as a rule folks do not adjust their refrigerator shelving which leads to tucking and shoving. This is how it gets cluttered. You should have one shelf tall enough for milk, juice and other bottled drinks. You may buy in bulk so this shelf can also have tall jars. Do not put the mayonnaise back on this shelf. If you do not put condiments and sauces in the door, make sure you have a shelf just for them. Also be sure you have a shelf at the proper height for leftover containers.

When returning food to the shelves, do not return food that has been left over for any longer than three days. Do not return any partially used packages of food either. Make sure all foods that are returned are in sealed or covered containers to prevent spills and odors. Add a box of baking soda in the back of the refrigerator which will help keep absorb odors.

Master Plan for the Crisper Drawers –(Fruits and Vegetable storage)

- Empty the drawers one at a time starting at the bottom.
- Clean and dry the drawer.
- Only place fresh foods back in the drawer.
- If it is looking like it is going bad or needs to be eaten tonight, leave it out.
- Make sure you place the foods that need to be eaten immediately in the top drawers and those that can have a few days in the bottom drawers.

Master Plan for Refrigerator Doors

- Depending on the type of refrigerator you have you will need to adjust the shelves on the door to fit your needs.
- Put the tall items like wine bottles on the bottom out of view
- Smaller bottles like the fancy mustards and horseradish towards the top.

- Check expiration dates prior to returning any jars to the door.

The Pantry

- Clear out the pantry all at once. All shelves.
- Start by setting your timer for 30 minutes. Sort foods by canned, packets, opened packages, foods you use regularly, and one time purchases.
- Throw away anything that is opened, such as marshmallows, chips, cookies, pasta, and seasoning packets.
- Toss away old cleaning supplies.
- Consolidate containers of things and get rid of what you don't use.
- Sort through your kitchen linens.
- Be sure not to have dingy, torn, dish towels, old sponges, and dishrags on display in the kitchen. Throw them out and replace them.

Cabinets

- Decluttering your cabinets needs to be done one cabinet at a time.
- Clean the shelves.

- Then check for chipped or cracked wares.
- Get rid of any cup or glass that is not part of a set.
- Pair up Tupperware with their lids.
- Get rid of broken sets unless they are large mixing bowls.
- Plastic Tupperware has to be replaced after a while.
- If the plastic is chewed, stained, has holes, smells bad, or is discolored, you need to throw it away.

Kitchen Appliances

- Get rid of all appliances off your countertop with the exception of toaster ovens that are used regularly or appliances that don't fit in your cabinets.
- Donate or recycle any appliance that you never use.
- The items you rarely use should be placed in the cupboards at the bottom, and those that you use regularly should be placed towards the top.

Bathrooms

- Toss outdated medicines –This could be dangerous if you don't. Do not flush unused or outdated medications down the toilet. Medications should not be stored in the bathroom due to the humidity that is often present. You will need to consolidate, for example you don't need 3 opened boxes of cotton swabs. Put them in one box or container together. Try to organize by placing all similar items in the same area.

- Toiletries —Be realistic. If you have extra bars of unused soap, this can be donated to local shelters. If the bottle of shampoo is empty, throw it out or refill it with new. Don't clutter your home with bottles that have no purpose. Remember there are organizations that need unused toiletries. Start purchasing soaps, shampoos, and conditioners the entire family can use.

- Make up —Mascara should be tossed out after 3-6 months and never shared. Old lipstick that you never use and pressed makeup is often needed by women's shelters. Go through everything and be sure to organize your drawer with lipsticks and makeup that you use. Remember if it doesn't look great on you and make you feel great, donate or throw it out.

Bedrooms

How many clothes do you really need? Show no mercy when going through your clothes. Questions to ask?

DECLUTTER GUIDE

1. Do you love it?
2. Do you wear it?
3. Does it project the image I want to show the world?
4. Does it itch or scratch?
5. Do they pinch my toes?
6. Are they too high to walk in?
7. Have they gone out of style and are never coming back?

Have 3 bins in your bedroom and your timer when you start the process. Anything that is old, torn, you don't wear; too small or outdated (donate). Have a bin labeled (excellent-good condition for consignment shops) and another bin labeled (torn or needs repair). Some agencies only want gently worn items, and others will take everything you have. This will save time so you don't have to stop and sort everything again.

- Do the same with accessories like jewelry, purses, shoes, scarfs and ties. If it isn't exciting to wear and your style anymore…don't be afraid to MOVE ON and donate.

- Remember; get rid of anything in your bedroom that doesn't belong there.

Closets & Drawers

Getting the clutter out of your closet and drawers needs to be a quick and easy process. It is a difficult task for many reasons. Usually we "tuck" & "stuff" in these locations. When we go to clean them we find new treasures and "stuff" we have forgotten about.

When deciding what to toss and what to keep ask: the 4 basic questions about every piece of clothing, shoes and accessory in your closet. Be brutal and if you can't, ask your friend or family member to lend a helping hand.

Keep a tote for anything that is not stained or discolored that you decide to eliminate. You can either donate or consign it and make a couple of bucks.

Here are the questions you need to remind yourself about every item in your closet:

1. Do you love it?
2. Do you wear it?
3. Does it project the image I want to show the world?
4. Does it make you feel good?

The Process

- Turn on your uplifting music.

- Start at the bottom of your closet.

- Remove anything from your closet that isn't clothing or shoes and accessories.

- Items such as luggage and other infrequently used items may be returned at a later time.

- Vacuum it well.

- Keep totes ready for getting rid of things.

- Set your timer for 20 minutes. As you go to place everything back on the bottom of the closet, remember to ask yourself the 4 basic questions about each article of clothing. The minute a negative answer comes up that would imply to get rid of it, toss it in the tote. Be sure you adhere strictly to your timetable and do not second guess yourself.

- Next take a quick glance at your clothing. Anything you notice right away remove from the hanger and put it in the tote.

- Now, set your timer for 15 minutes if you have a large closet. Start with the rods and place your hand on each item. In three seconds, you know whether you want to keep it. Go with your immediate yes or no. Remember you have to make a decision because you are moving quickly. Once again be brutal with your decision and stick by it.

- Finally, repeat the last exercise with your shelves allowing only 5 minutes.

Drawers

- Set your timer to 5 minutes per drawer. Your family junk drawer gets 15 minutes.

- Start by emptying a drawer. Do not do all of them together. Take it one drawer at a time in case you get overwhelmed.

- Clean it out well and decide what you will put back in it.

- Remove anything you consider junk from the drawer and discard.

- Next set your timer for fifteen minutes. Put anything you want to keep in the drawer back in it and put the other stuff in a box to donate or sell.

- Take a few minutes, after you have decided what to keep, and arrange it nicely back in the drawer.

- Take a plastic shoe box and place all your sealed packets in it after checking expiration dates.

Home office / Desk

One of the best ways to declutter your desk is to start all over. You can use the timer and allow yourself one hour. Give yourself ample time to complete the task. Take a picture of your desk so you can see where your trouble spots lie. Then take everything off your desk and put it in boxes.

Go through the boxes and decide what you need on your desk. Anything you don't want discard. Only keep the things you need, not the things you might need. The next thing is you need to give your desk a working order.

Move things across your desk from left to right which is a natural order. Find a place for everything. Do not create a pile of "stuff" to put away later. The best way to keep a decluttered desk is to place similar items together. This helps to expedite the process.

Take a look at the picture you took. Have you identified your trouble spots? If you have a tendency to stack papers in a particular place find a container and place it there so the papers stay contained. You will want to invest in some eye-catching organizational tools. It helps to label everything as you go. You can invest in a label maker or create stickers as you go.

Hide your computer cords or go wireless! Whenever possible, hide your cords in a cord manager and label them. You might want to check out <u>Omni mount cable management system</u> on Amazon or check out <u>Signum cable management</u> from IKEA.

There are countless ideas out there to tame the cables so be sure to not procrastinate and select a system so you can get this done.

Finally, never leave your desk dirty at the end of the day. Give everything a home and put everything in its place at the end of the day. Be sure to schedule daily (10 minutes) or a weekly desk clean up task so everything stays organized.

Decluttering the Garage, Basement and Attic

- Depending on the amount of clutter in these areas, you may want to set the timer to only allow yourself any 2 of these areas on a day that you have more time. You may for example, initially set your timer for 2.5 hours to tackle your basement, take a break and then 2.5 hours for the garage.

- Be sure to have upbeat music on with plenty of water and snacks available. This will help to maintain your energy levels.

- Once you make the initial commitment to complete the task (or at least get started), you are in a better position to evaluate how effective this method was for you. For example, you may need to break the job up into mini-jobs if you do not have an entire afternoon or day to devote to the project. Safety is critical when going through these areas of your home due to the weight of many items. You may want to have a friend or family members with you to assist with the tasks.

- Use 2 very large containers with labels (Trash) or (Donate) and clear out a place on one side of the room to place these containers. You can also get garbage bags and don't forget your timer, markers, and tape.

- Donate all tools you don't use regularly. Remember you don't need 8 of the same kind of pliers or screwdrivers. You can create a small tool kit for certain areas such as the kitchen, or car.

- Purchase shelving and waterproof storage boxes --such as plastic totes --to store items in an organized fashion and get everything off the floor. Shelving comes in a variety of prices and can be found in plastic, metal or wood.

- If you haven't already you may want to invest in space-saving wall mounted systems. This helps to make sure you make the maximum use of your wall space and get everything off the floor. Keep in mind you are not investing in cute containers to hide items in these area, just to organize the essentials. Donate and sell what you don't need. Don't keep items just for a "rainy day". If you don't need the items it's time to purge.

- Go through storage containers currently and remove the contents and sort. You may need to use markers to note what is in the box, and stack the waterproof boxes on the shelving. You can assign each box with a number and note the contents.

- Clean out all cupboards and closets. Be sure to sweep or vacuum the area.

- Toss old paint that is unusable, newspapers, or items that have decayed. You can donate unused chemicals and old exercise equipment.

- Sort through old boxes of memories. Do you really need your report card from the 3rd grade? Do you need the ticket stub from your first date in college?

DON'T FORGET YOUR FREE BONUSES

https://dl.bookfunnel.com/2dximykla1

Review Week 1 – Section 2

- Now that you have read what you should do during your first week of decluttering let's take a look at the highlights!

  - **Needed Supplies:**
    Garbage Bags and Garbage
    Totes, Boxes, or Bins
    A Close Friend or Family Member
    Music
    Get A Timer

- **Tips For Making It Through The Process**

  Move quickly through the processes…don't give yourself time to second guess
  Stick to the time limits you set…this is your first step towards discipline
  Keep things neat as you go, some areas will require you spread out a bit
  Keep in mind what the area is being used for
  Keep your eye on the prize

- **Last Thoughts**

If it is taking you too long to go through a room, and you find it hard to make or stick to a decision just walk away for a while. Remember this is new for you and you may feel a bit overwhelmed. Changing habits isn't easy. The processes are designed so you can take small bits but to move you through very quickly so you don't fall back into old habits of keeping things you don't need.

SECTION 3

Week 2 - Your Finances And Your Life

Now that you have made it through your first week and have found solutions to old issues, it is time to move on to an area that seems to be a little more difficult to change. But, have faith in yourself...you can do this.

Cleaning up your home first was imperative so that you could feel the liberation of decluttering. Remember the feeling of how it felt to just sit in a room that had been wiped clean of the clutter? Do you remember being able to breathe? You may have even taken a few deep breaths and just sat there enjoying the feeling. Do you remember sitting there thinking "what do I do now"? Strange wasn't it?

Once the "stuff" had been removed you just sat and it felt odd as though you should be doing something, but you didn't know what. What you felt was the liberating feeling of decluttering. Remember that feeling as you move forward because it is about to get better!

As you move toward decluttering your finances and life, keep in mind that you are on your way to freeing up time and energy so you can gain control over your life.

Shred & Ditch the Paper

Buy yourself a scanner and a shredder! There is no reason to hang onto the old paper. You can also get yourself an external hard drive to store all your financials. Most people have a hard time keeping track of important paperwork. But getting rid of paper and organizing your financials on a separate hard drive you will save you time, lessen stress and help you feel at ease instead of panicking when you have to get your hands on documents you need.

To make the process go easier and to give you some guidelines here are a few tips to get you on your way.

1. Start with old documents. Things like old bills, credit card, and bank statements. Check with the companies to be sure you can access your account information online. If you can be sure to shred all the old documents.

2. You need to organize receipts for taxes and warranties. Make a folder on your extra hard drive for each and scan the receipts. Organize them so that they make sense to you. Keep it simple so it is easy to access them when needed.

3. Medical & dental bills and receipts should all be scanned and kept in a separate file so you can use them later on your taxes for a deduction if you itemize.

4. Life Insurance policies should be shredded and discarded if you no longer have the policies. If you still have the policies, it is a good idea to hang onto the original signature pages, but go ahead and scan the policy and applications and then shred those documents.

5. Any investment paperwork should be scanned and just like your life insurance policies, keep the signature pages and shred the rest.

Here is a chart you can print and hang in your office for a quick and easy reference. It will help you with how long you should retain your records.

Few Days
Receipts for ATM's & Bank Deposits
Grocery Receipts & Minor Purchases

Monthly
Receipts for Credit Card Purchases Or Credit Card Statements With Non-Tax Related Expenses

Yearly
(Unless Needed For Taxes)
Check Stubs
Brokerage/Mortgage Statements
Medical & Dental Bills

7 Years
Supporting Documents For Tax Returns

Indefinately
Tax Returns; IRS Forms for IRA's or Roth; Retirement & Brokerage Annual Statements; Home Improvement Receipts (Until You Sell The Home), Receipts For Large Purchases For Insurance

Bill Consolidation

Bill consolidation is an amazing way to cut down on your financial clutter. There are several ways you can start consolidating your bills. While some may take a little research and some creative ingenuity, the benefits you will reap from bill consolidation can help you rest at ease. There are a few ways you can consolidate your bills and save money. All these ways to follow will help to declutter your life with paperwork, lessen your debt, save you money, and make it easier to monitor your finance. You will also decrease your stress levels and increase your freedom.

Services

This one is a bit of common sense, but you would be amazed at how you may overlook it. Get rid of services you don't use. Many people subscribe to magazines and then lose interest. Out of habit, they continue to just pay the bill. Another example of this would be movie channels or services. Why pay for cable if you don't really watch TV. Or maybe you could downgrade and pay less. You may also consider getting rid of movie services like Hulu if all you watch is Netflix.

Bundling

Bundling your services is a very cost effective way to declutter. Many companies now have packages that allow you to combine your TV, phone and internet; or combine your water, sewer and garbage; maybe even combine your electric and gas bills. Research your local companies to see how many services you can combine. Many times it will come with a substantial savings. With that savings you are cutting out one or two statements per bundle. That's a lot of clutter.

Some things we may not think of bundling would be IRA's or retirement accounts. If you have worked a few different places you may have accumulated a few retirement accounts such as 401K's. A good idea would be to look at your accounts and find out which one gets the best rate. You could roll all the accounts into one. Another way to consolidate these accounts would be to see if your current bank offers better rates on IRA's or 401K's. Be sure to consult your accountant or tax advisor before you make changes to your accounts to avoid fees or penalties for rolling over accounts.

Pay Down Debt & Carry Fewer Credit Cards

Pay off all those little bills. The best way to do this is to pay the minimum payment on all your bills but choose a couple to over pay on. Start with the small ones. As you free up your life of your smaller bills and clear the clutter of communications from those companies, you will find you have more resources for the larger ones.

When you have so many small accounts, you can't make headway. Your finances are spread very thin, and it becomes difficult to track. Once you knock out the little ones, you can take the resources you would have used on them and make bigger payments on the larger bills. Before you know it you will be down to just a few bills beyond your basic living expenses and on your way to financial freedom.

Carrying fewer credit cards is also a good idea. The fewer cards you carry, the less debt you will incur. You will also eliminate the possibility of missing payments for accounts you lose track of. By carrying fewer cards, you will also eliminate mail or email and make it easier to monitor your finances. Be sure to check which cards you have had the longest and the cards with the best interest rates. You want to be sure not to damage your credit and save money by keeping cards with the lowest interest rates.

Consolidating Credit Cards

If you are trying to make an immediate difference and don't want to wait for the long process of paying off debt, another option would be consolidation. Many companies offer 0% on balance transfers from other cards. So you can get anywhere from 6 months to 12 months interest free.

You can do one of two things to save some money. You can take your cards with high interest rates and consolidate onto one of these zero interest cards or you can take cards with small balances and combine onto zero interest cards. Either way you are saving on interest payments and you are minimize the accounts you have to monitor.

If you travel frequently consider a credit card that rewards you. If you pay the balance off each month, there are cards you can use accumulate a significant amount of points. You will have to shop around to find the best credit cards for your lifestyle.

Automate Savings & Start-Up Bill Pay

Another way to streamline your finances so that you come out ahead would be to automate your savings. Direct deposit of your paycheck can help with this. Designate a portion of your check and have it deposited straight into your savings account. While you are at it you can even have additional amounts automatically deposited into your retirement accounts.

Many banking institutions offer an automatic bill pay that you can take advantage of. There are several ways automatic bill pay can help to streamline your finances. By setting up a system, you will have the convenience of making sure your regular bills are taken care of. The more you can set up the better.

Automatic Bill Pay can help with your credit score. By having regularly scheduled payments to companies that report to credit agencies, you can establish a record of paying your bills on time without having the stress of having to monitor and worry about the payment yourself. Automatic bill pay reduces your risk of missing payments or being delinquent with payments.

Another advantage of automatic bill pay is that it can help to reduce the chances of identity theft. By limiting where your personal information is you reduce the risk of theft. While online payments present a certain amount of risk, it is far less than sending your account information out via public means such as the mail.

Finally, automatic bill pay saves you time and money. You will be spending less time monitoring and worrying about your bills. This will give you time to think of the things that are more important. This method of paying your bills reduces the risk of delinquency and saves you from having to pay late fees. There will no longer be a need for envelopes, stamps, and checks. Better yet, you will save money on gas from not having to go to pay bills or unnecessary trips to the post office.

Commitments

A clear indicator that you are overcommitting on your time commitments is when you lack desire or have anxiety about going to meetings, appointments, or events. Whether you overcommit due to the inability to say no, over planning, or unrealistic ideas of our personal capabilities the stress it causes can produce physical symptoms such as muscle, back, and neck stiffness. It can also produce headaches. The ideal solution is saying "no".

So how do you cut back when you feel you have to do everything you have committed to and you feel as though you can't back out? The first thing you need to do is to settle in and relax. Clear your head and breathe. Just relax and think about the things you have committed to. Make a list of all the commitments you have.

The Process

Take a look at your personal calendar and start by penciling in time for the commitments that are deal breakers, the ones you can't give up. Examples would include picking up the kids, taking a moment for yourself, maybe you take care of an elderly parent and you have times you checked on them.

Then take a look at the time you have left. You need to set limits for what can be achieved in the time you have left. If on Monday, you have three hours during the day where you do not have family commitments or personal time, you may want to limit your activities for that time period to one or two small errands or projects.

Next take the list of all the commitments you made and prioritize them. Which ones are the ones you need to get done? This isn't necessarily the most urgent, but the ones that will have the biggest and lasting effect on you and your family.

Look at the ones you have left. Which commitments can you change? Do you have commitments for children's functions that can be changed to other days or times? Maybe you have doctor or dentist appointments that can be changed to days where you have larger blocks available. Look for commitments that you can ask other people to help with.

Finally, find those commitments that you can just graciously get out of all together. The goal is to ultimately rearrange your schedule so that you have free time. Time to do things you enjoy doing. Be sure you allow yourself this downtime to refresh and rejuvenate so you can be ready for the next round of commitments. Pick a couple of days where you commit to yourself not to schedule activities leaving you time to spend quality time with yourself and your family.

Block this time out on your calendar. Make sure you schedule it like everything else and this time becomes your nonnegotiable time. Within the first week of scheduling this time you will notice a substantial difference in your emotional and physical well-being.

Routines

When you hear the word routine, do you cringe? Its okay if you do, most people do. However, establishing routines does not have to be dull and boring, and they certainly can save you time and money. You can even get your family involved. Routines are a way of making sure you get those things done in your life that need to get done. I remember when I was little, my mother would get up every Friday morning and do her deep cleaning for the weekend like scrubbing the bathrooms and detailing the car.

Once you establish a routine, it can become a habit, and you are able to accomplish your weekly necessities without even thinking about it. They can change your life from chaos to well-managed.

A few examples of routines might be to do your laundry on a set day or a couple of days if you have a lot and making sure it is done from start to finish. Taking the laundry straight from the dryer and putting it away right away can save you time by not having to iron wrinkled clothes. A routine like this can save you money too. By having regular laundry days, you aren't running out frantically buying socks and underwear because the laundry isn't done.

Having dinner together every night to catch up with family events might be a new routine to establish. This routine can be a way of being informed of new activities or commitments which family members are considering. You might even try doing dishes right after dinner as a way of enlisting help to get the chore done and extend family time to the kitchen.

Once a routine is established it isn't set in stone. It can be changed and modified so that it works for you and your family. Setting new routines is easy. Take a look at the infographic.

It is a simple 5 step process that will become second nature once you get used to using it. It can help you save time and money by creating routines that are efficient and help keep you from spending money unnecessarily.

Identify An Issue: Brainstorm to decide what problem it is you need to solve. (I.e.: Chaotic getting out of the house in the morning, hard keeping the house clean, or dinner is always late.

Set A Goal: Think about what it is you want to accomplish. Be specific. Some goals might be getting out of the house on time, making sure visible living spaces are ready for company or getting dinner on the table by 6:00 pm.

Create A Plan: Think about sets of behaviors that linked together will accomplish your goal. Set shoes by the door, lay out your clothes the night before, prepare lunch for the next day, pack a bag for the next day and set it by your shoes, and lay clothes out the night before.

Troubleshoot Potential Problems: An example might be laundry not completed, so that no clean clothes are available to wear.

Take a Test Drive: Once you have ironed out the kinks of your plan, and you have determined possible obstacles, take it for a test drive. Try it out and see how it fits.

Computer

While cleaning off your desk seems simple enough, cleaning or organizing your computer will be a little trickier. It will take a bit more time as well. In order to do a good job, you will need a flash drive and a printer.

- Start by getting rid of any programs you don't use. Go to your control panel and open your programs. Uninstall anything you do not use. If you look, and you don't know what it is, look it up and see if it is essential to the operations of your computer.

- Next go through each of your files. Delete anything you no longer need. If it is something you need to keep, store it on a flash drive or print it off and delete the file from your computer.

- Next go through and organize your documents into folders you can recognize. Music and pictures should be kept separate from documents.

- Finally, run a disk clean up. You can access it through your system tools. Running regular checks and cleanups will keep your computer in good working condition.

Digital Clutter

Digital clutter can be the most time-consuming clutter. It comes in the form of free downloads, emails, unused or disorganized computer files, text messages, social media notifications, digital e-mails, and much more. This form of clutter is the most overwhelming and time sucking kind of clutter. The disorganization and distraction are dangerous because it is subtle and occurs over the course of time. Sometimes if you are very active digitally, it can happen quickly without notice.

E-mail

Often times if you don't keep up on it, you can have thousands of emails to sift through. It also is time-consuming to go through hundreds of emails a day because you signed up to receive a free offer. If you do not use a large server, you should get one especially, if you have multiple e-mail accounts. By using the larger servers, you can have your email forwarded to one location, so you do not have to log into all those accounts.

Go through and create folders in your inbox for the newsletters you want to keep or read. You can also create folders for personal and clients. If you use a large email server like Google, AOL, or Yahoo, you will be able to create rules for how you email is handled once it is delivered to your inbox. You can set up rules that will automatically deliver your newsletters to their folders so they can wait for you until you have the opportunity to look at them.

Any newsletters, offers, or people you no longer want to receive messages from you should unsubscribe from their list. This will help to keep your inbox from getting overwhelming. Once you get your email under control, it shouldn't take any more than 10 minutes a day to read your important email. You should check out unrollme.com . This program can help you tremendously with email management. I'm sure there are others available, but this is the one that I use and recommend.

When handling your inbox, there are only three things you should do with your emails act on it, file it, or delete it. This will keep your email task manageable.

Social Media

A huge digital time and energy drainer is social media. If you have several accounts, you should look into a software or online platform that allows you to group them all into one location. There are quite a few online programs that can do this for you. If you look into social media managing platforms, you will find some that are free to use.

Here you can post and respond to posts all in one location for multiple social media accounts. This prevents you from getting stuck in one media account for too long. You can also schedule your posts to go out ahead of time, so you free up time to do other things. This may sound silly for a personal account, but it really does help.

Just think...you can remember all the wonderful things your family did over the weekend and send them to family and friends over the course of a day instead of posting all at once. You can also take a few minutes to respond to those who may have left notes on your Facebook, Pinterest, and Twitter all at once.

Paper Mail

Another form of information you should try to streamline should be your snail mail. A good rule of thumb is to place a basket or container in a permanent place.

All your mail should stay there until you go through it. As a rule of thumb you should concentrate on touching your mail only once. Open your mail and then file until you need it like your bills. Once it is opened it either needs to be filed or thrown away. Junk mail should hit the garbage and never make it to your mail container.

File Cabinet

Final Advice is your file cabinet. If you are saying what file cabinet…you should probably get one!! Most homes can get by with a small two drawer cabinet. That gives you one drawer for personal paperwork and bills and one drawer for warranties for tools, appliances, and machinery.

If you have a file cabinet, you should empty the drawers and organize the drawers as mentioned above. Go through each folder and either trash outdated documents or file them in a cardboard file box if you have to keep them. Your home file cabinet should have documents that are no older than 5 years old. Your warranty information should not be kept past its time unless you have it attached to the owner's manual. The owner's manuals should be discarded once the item is no longer in use at your home.

Week 3 Review

Here are the highlights of your second week.

- Get rid of the paper – be sure to scan the important receipts and document and keep paper copies of signature pages. Follow the guidelines of other important documents.

- Consolidate bills through eliminating unnecessary services, bundling services, pay down debt, and automate your finances. Take a look at your commitments and get rid of the commitments that you can or don't especially want to do.

- Set routines to help you and your family save time and reduce the feelings of chaos and anxiety.

Last Thoughts

Remember that the goal of decluttering is to simplify your life. The process will help you determine the things in your life that are important and those that are not, but somehow have been made to seem more important than they really are. Know by completing the process you will regain control of your life, eliminate stress and anxiety, and make time to rest and do the things you love to do!

SECTION 4

The Long Haul

The key to living a decluttered life is setting up routines and processes to help you maintain a lifestyle without "stuff". The following processes are simple ways to help you keep your life tidy, so you don't have to waste money or time.

Create Central Locations

- Make sure that when you are looking for ways to maintain your clutter that you create locations to keep your stuff. Look for decorative bins, bulletin boards, anything that will help you keep things in check. A wonderful idea is to create central locations for the everyday things.

- An example might be to get an attractive key rack that has a nice shelf which can double as a central docking station for all your electronics. In the morning all your necessities are in one place. This eliminates the chaos or feelings of being scattered in the morning as you hunt for your keys or phone.

- In our home, our shoes are kept in a nice basket near the door along with a rack for coats, hats, and bags. Shoes come off, and socks are put on or a pair of slippers when it is colder. Not only are we not chasing shoes, but it cuts down on the number of times the floors are swept and vacuumed.
- We now only sweep and mop once a week! It is fabulous! We are never hunting for backpacks or coats because they are all nicely stored near the door.

Mail and Communication

- Consider a family communication center. Whether your family is 2 or twelve, this idea will benefit you. A wall calendar is ideal for everyone to write in their activities, and a bulletin board for a visual schedule can work well in a busy home. This keeps everything neat and clean, so everyone knows what is going on.
- Every night before your week begins, take a peek and discard any messages you no longer need and place times and locations for the next week on the calendar. Simple rule to follow if it isn't on the calendar, it doesn't get done!

Put Things In Their Place

- It is really easy to leave your hair brush on the counter or leave breakfast dishes in the sink. The best system to keeping things from cluttering up your home is to use the old adage, "a place for everything and everything in its place."

- Make it a habit when you are finished using something put it back where you got it. This is true for everything in your home.

- If you think this is too much for you, you can always practice a reset rule. Before you go to bed, make a sweep around the house. Allow yourself about 15 –20 minutes. Run through all the rooms in your house and put everything back where it goes.

- You can make this a routine and engage the whole family and cut down your time considerably by making family members responsible for specific zones in the house. For example, 10 minutes before bed the kids are responsible for their bedrooms, playroom and their own bathrooms.

- Another idea to help you stay on top of clutter is to create a clutter box. When you go through your home on your check take a small box with you that you can easily carry. Anything in your check area that is not in its place, put in the box.

- Make family members responsible for checking the clutter box for their belongings. Anything left in the box over a week is discarded. This makes family responsible for their things. You'll be amazed at how the box becomes too large over time.

Clean Regularly – Especially The Hot Spots

You are very aware of the "Hot Spots" in your home. In my sister's home, I've noticed it is the kitchen counter, the dining room table, and the living room coffee tables. Everything gets placed here. Mail, projects that are worked on, purses, wallets, cell phones, empty microwave popcorn bags, drinking glasses, and the list is endless.

These are the "lived in" spots. Make it a habit, every time you walk by one of these locations you pick up, straighten or de-clutter the area. It takes just an extra few seconds and keeps these areas from getting out of hand. Then no matter what your "hot spots" will be clean and clutter-free.

Recycle & Donate

- This idea is wonderful except beware, it is the hardest to get accomplished. Most people are not very good about getting rid of the things we acquire. For this reason, you need to make a weekly trip to donate all items in the bin that is labeled to donate. This way you are not accumulating donated items or start taking the items out of the bin to justify a reason to keep the item.

- Have your family members place things in the bin regularly that they no longer want or need. Be sure to keep the bins sorted: Gently used or Needs repair. In order to get folks on board remind them when they donate their used or gently used belongings, they are helping out people in need. This includes toys and games!

- What a better way to give back to your community. In order to drive the idea home, take your kids with you the first time so they can see how much their efforts are appreciated. It will help with the system at home. Before you know it, they will be getting rid of things you never thought they would.

Keep Up On Expiration Dates

This may seem like a no-brainer, but actually this is the one area people neglect the most. Make sure that you create a routine of setting aside one day a month to check for expired food, medications, and other perishables. Don't forget the man cave and regularly check this overlooked area.

Be sure that if you use the clutter box method you strictly adhere to the expiration date you set. Put this on your list of expires to check on a weekly or monthly basis.

Best Practices

Here is a list of some tips that were not discussed in detail but may help you on your path to a life with less stuff.

- **Cut Out The Shopping** – Such a bad phrase but true. If you don't need it, don't buy it.

- **Make A Habit to De-Clutter before The Holidays** – Before gift giving holidays, be sure to eliminate what you are replacing or giving.

- **Take A Picture** – Kids projects and sentimental items can be hung on the wall or laid out on a table. If you don't use them take a picture and discard the items.

- **One In And One Out** – Every time you purchase something once you have de-cluttered be sure to get rid of an item.

- **Clean The Fridge On Shopping Day** – Be sure to clean out old food and replace it with the fresh.

- **Give Yourself An Allowance** – Take the money you can live on for the week and do just that. Train yourself to cut out impulse buying.

- **Create A Maybe Box** – Put things in you're not sure you'll need, if you don't need them in a week get rid of them.

- **Learn To Say No!** – Do not over commit and if you don't need it, it is okay to say no thank you.

- **Make Lists** – Make lists of the things you need to buy or do. Be strict about the list and don't do anything not on the list.

- **Don't Be Afraid To Try Again** – If de-cluttering didn't work right away don't give up. Remember perfection is not the goal, but setting up systems to help organize and evaluate what you actually need can help relieve a lot of tension and stress.

Conclusion

The quest for living a more purposeful and more organized life has become a major concern for many people. There has been no magical solution discovered or set of rules to follow. However, research has proven that clutter has such a profound effect on our mental capacities which leaves us exhausted.

Taking steps to change your way of thinking and getting rid of the clutter that surrounds you can be difficult at the beginning. **The Declutter Guide—How to organize your life in 2 weeks or less; Organizing tips to simplify your life**, has tried to provide you with guidelines to make the process more streamlined.

Hopefully you have identified why you clutter and have decided on an action plan utilizing some or all of the strategies outlined. Without your determination and drive to implement the strategies, nothing will change. When you look to keep your life de-cluttered don't forget it is a work in progress. Don't give up if you don't get it right the first time. Our homes and lives cannot by any means be standardized. Take small steps and remember what you learned...

- Start decluttering your home by reviewing your living spaces and decide a day of the week and a timeframe to handle that space before you move on to the next area.

- Create central locations where you can group the things that are important but make your house messy and cluttered.

- Find ways to put things back where they belong. The key is put them away right away.

- Find your family's "hot spots" and clean those places regularly.

- Recycle & Donate – Help others out with your excess.

- Keep a close eye on your perishables both in your home and in your garage

- If at first you don't succeed try again until you find a fit.

The life you will have once you de-clutter and maintain it will be liberating. You will begin to enjoy doing things without the anxiety of all your clutter baggage. You will find you have, less stress and anxiety, more energy, and best of all feel in control of your life.

Latest Book Release

If you find yourself feeling down, filled with worry and self-doubt you can check out my latest book, "Feeling Good Now ! How to Be Happy and Find Inner Peace in 30 Days"

This book is a journey of learning how to find your power, manage anxiety, and uncover your true potential with actionable steps: Be sure to visit happinessinnerpeace.com for more details.

Don't Forget Some of the Best things in Life are FREE!!

Be sure to Get Your FREE Declutter Checklists & Copy of PRESENT MOMENT
https://dl.bookfunnel.com/2dximykla1

A Plea to Your Very Generous Nature

If you have found this guide helpful in any way and you like what you read, would you consider going to Amazon or your favorite book outline and leaving a review? The process is a lot easier than you think and I will be grateful.

Keep in mind, I know you are busy and I thank you for your kind words.

Sincerely,
Ariel Benet Savant

About the Author

The journey to becoming an author began when I was working in the corporate world. I felt corporate America had a lot of restrictions, pressures, and aggravation, so I started writing short stories and creating mandala drawings in my spare time. I found that no matter how busy I was, I could find some moments of peace by doing this. After losing my job, I started to publish my work and several months later began writing full time. I've never looked back.

When I'm not writing, I enjoy spending time with my spouse, family, close friends, and our Yorkie whose name is Toby. We are very passionate about helping people and are involved in a number of charitable organizations. We are fortunate to spend a lot of time in nature which is where I find inspiration to create mandala drawings.

I enjoy reading good books especially thrillers and crime novels, listening to classical music, and hiking among the many trails near our home.

Follow Ariel on Twitter @arielbsavant

Become a Fan on Facebook

Check out Ariel's latest Book Trailers on You-Tube

Author Website: www.arielsavant.com

www.ingramcontent.com/pod-product-compliance
Lightning Source LLC
Chambersburg PA
CBHW050444010526
44118CB00013B/1671